Necessary Breaking Points:

STAYING CONNECTED WITH GOD DURING CRISES

Frances, P. Wilson

WESTBOW
PRESS®
A DIVISION OF THOMAS NELSON
& ZONDERVAN

This book is a work of non-fiction. Unless otherwise noted, the author and the publisher make no explicit guarantees as to the accuracy of the information contained in this book and in some cases, names of people and places have been altered to protect their privacy.

Scripture taken from the New King James Version. Copyright © 1979, 1980, 1982 by Thomas Nelson, Inc. Used by permission. All rights reserved.

WestBow Press books may be ordered through booksellers or by contacting:

WestBow Press
A Division of Thomas Nelson & Zondervan
1663 Liberty Drive
Bloomington, IN 47403
www.westbowpress.com
1 (866) 928-1240

Because of the dynamic nature of the Internet, any web addresses or links contained in this book may have changed since publication and may no longer be valid. The views expressed in this work are solely those of the author and do not necessarily reflect the views of the publisher, and the publisher hereby disclaims any responsibility for them.

Any people depicted in stock imagery provided by Thinkstock are models, and such images are being used for illustrative purposes only. Certain stock imagery © Thinkstock.

ISBN: 978-1-5127-3318-1 (sc)
ISBN: 978-1-5127-4214-5 (e)

Library of Congress Control Number: 2016903298

Print information available on the last page.

WestBow Press rev. date: 05/02/2016

Contents

Biographical Information

Current Position: Companion Aid, Dementia Care

Educational background: Registered Nurse Diploma from Centennial College

Certificate in Biblical Studies from Ontario Bible College & Seminary (now Tyndale Seminary)

Writing course with Christian Writer's Guild

One poem published in 2011: Stars in Their Hearts

One Poem: 2013 Who's who in Poetry

One article published in 2015 in Living Abundant

Church Affiliation: member of the Associated Gospel Churches of Canada

Served as a cross-cultural missionary Nurse in Niger, West Africa 1994 to 2007

CHAPTER 1

The heat is on

Although it may not be immediately obvious, or even obvious at all, everything including inanimate objects, is in the process of change. Some changes affect the life cycle and would cause concern if they did not occur. From Biology classes, I recall that living things grow and move. Growth is an example of change. Imagine Iris bulbs remaining bulbs, or your dog at three years old, still making puppy mistakes. They need to change, and those are necessary changes.

Change is crucial, but before some changes occur, matters must reach the breaking point: "The moment of crisis in a situation."[1] Another recall: water freezes at 0^0 Celsius, and boils at 212^0 Fahrenheit. In both cases, water reaches a point of drastic change, but remains water in other forms. Each form determines function, and has benefits. The discovery that water freezes, led to the creation of refrigeration, and that development has revolutionized life for everyone.

Cooking, another kind of change, "was first used as preservation. It's the process by which we produce safe and edible food."[2] We combine unpalatable items, sometimes with herbs and spices, and usually apply heat, creating something palatable, but of more importance, safe for consumption. The meat in particular, must reach that point, lest its consumption harm, rather than help. Like water in frozen and steam states, the meat and vegetables are in another state, and heat is the change agent.

Fever is a change agent which alerts the body to invasion and acts like one of its defense mechanisms. When it reaches a certain point, it necessitates intervention and although the sensation is unpleasant, it prevents invading microbes from making damaging changes in the body. Before medical advancement: "The fever is broken" evoked smiles and sighs of relief. In its process, fever indicates the need for changes, and may force us to make some changes in health, or in overall living habits.

God works in similar ways. He may allow and use situations in our lives to alert and sensitize us to changes we may need to make. We are His vessels, and His property. Paul reminds us: "We are His workmanship, created in Christ Jesus for good works, which He ordained for us to walk in."[3] However, we lost that ability through our marred relationship, just like silver articles lose their glow due to tarnish. Sin is that tarnish. Therefore, we cannot be of use to God just as we are. This may sound like a contradiction to the popular stance that God loves us just as we are. Yes, He does love us in our sins, but such love compels us to strive to be like him – pure and holy.

None of us would use tarnished silverware. Instead we apply polish to bring out the glow. Neither would we use soiled articles. Rather, we separate, then wash them before we even think of using them. God hates sin, and will not tolerate it. He deals with our sins and seeks to restore His likeness in us. Meanwhile, He sets us aside until He cleanses us. We retain some idiosyncrasies, characteristics, and personality traits, so sometimes God turns up the heat in order to change our incompatible behaviors. He's holy and commands us to be like Him, but often we're non-compliant, so He brings us to points in our lives where we become broken. We must reach those points before we attain the effectiveness He demands, just like foods, during cooking time, must reach a certain point, or before minerals become the gems we desire to see. In order to get our attention, God may use seemingly drastic measures just like we use a product and a cloth to produce friction, and bring out the shine. It does not necessarily mean we have sinned, but often, that is the case.

Change includes stress, and even situations which delight us evoke stress. How much more so, will situations we'd rather avoid. Our temperaments affect our responses. We respond either with resignation tinged with bitterness, or allow the full effects of transforming changes. When we entertain in our homes, we polish the silverware – remove the tarnish. It's important to know that God always prepares us for service, and that usually involves some changes. We all admire beautiful things, and attaining that mark, requires work in many cases. For example, jewel experts tell us: "Pressure and heat change the minerals in rocks, into gems."[4]

Certain Biblical characters, childhood heroes from Sunday school lessons, needed polishing. In our immaturity as children, we esteemed them heroes, because we heard only about some acts of heroism, but as we mature, we discover their other sides, and learn that life surpasses heroism and perfectionism. We start relating on a deeper level; and learn from their lives, like Scripture states: "For whatever things were written before, were written for our learning, that we through the patience and comfort of the Scriptures might have hope."[5]

Moreover, their lives teach us about sin, and how to avoid it. They all needed to arrive at their breaking points. Other characters followed the rules – obeyed God, yet they too needed polishing. They too, needed to arrive at their breaking points. All Old Testament characters experienced trials, but six stand out: Jacob, Joseph, Moses, Hannah, Naomi and Ruth. Each case was different, but God had one specific purpose: preparation for service.

- How do you react to changes?

CHAPTER 2

"The gem cannot be polished without friction, nor people without trials."[6]

Jacob: From nose out of joint to hip out of joint

Jacob's problem began in utero; it was as though the twins were already tussling. "Two nations are in your womb. Expect some painful facts like separation, and be aware that one will outwit the other", Rebekah learned. Liberty allows us to imagine that she longed for the expected day of delivery. She already loved her babies, and could not wait to meet them, but her body was no match for the uterine battle. When the glad day arrived, Jacob was grabbing unto his brother's heels.

Names have significance, even more so in those days. It was not his fault that Jacob bore his. As though that was not enough, their parents perpetuated the problem, and their behavior produced heartaches which stemmed from rivalries, divisions, aggression and violence. Favoritism was the culprit. Isaac preferred Esau, Rebekah chose Jacob. Each parent's gender has significant roles which the other can never fulfill, so each boy probably schemed and vied to win the other parent's favor. Jacob probably put his nose out of joint, wishing he were Isaac's favorite. Likewise, Esau wished Rebekah included him in her favor. Esau was not without blame. He later caused them heartaches through his tendency to act contrary to their teaching and expectation. He also had a problem focusing, which had a domino effect. His failure to focus, affected his ability to prioritize, and consequently without much coercion, he traded something which he instead should have fought to maintain.

Hunger can mess up every system in our bodies including the nervous system, so hunger pangs might have influenced his decision. Instead of waiting for a solid meal, someone who is hungry may devour anything at hand. Even without hunger's influence some people eat dessert first, spoiling the appetite for a wholesome meal. Esau needed the food at the moment, but he traded significance for urgency. Jacob's problem, however, had more far reaching effects. He was the stronger of the twins, but he abused that strength. He manipulated situations so that he could get what he wanted. He took advantage of Esau's vulnerability. That behavior had a ripple-like effect. He deceived his twin, his father also, and, he deceived himself. Esau was hurt, and deserved sympathy, although he added to his own hurt. In that culture, it was a contradiction plus humiliation, if a younger sibling usurped the elder. Added to the misery, was the fact that the blessing he received was like cold left-overs, after everyone else enjoyed a warm, satisfying meal. The already fragile relationship weakened. Peace and contentment eluded Esau, as well as Rebekah.

Situations deteriorated and Rebekah observed everything with concern, and alerted and probably encouraged Jacob to protect himself. It soon reached the point where he had to make other living arrangements. There is a harshness when someone has to escape from those who should offer protection and shelter: family. Refugees also can verify the fact that it ruins the spirit, when someone has to get away from the place to which they should run from assaults: home. Such were the situations with Jacob, and although in his case, he helped to perpetuate the circumstances, one cannot help feeling a tinge of sorrow for him. He ran from Esau's anger, and revenge, and it appeared he had success. He went to live with his relatives, but that did not solve much, because the problem was rooted in his heart. So when he escaped from Esau, the problem remained. His, is an example of exchanging a bad situation for something worse: he 'jumped from the frying pan into the fire.'

Life with his relatives presented challenges. There was no dullness, but it was not all pleasantness either. Both sides practiced deception although they were probably unaware of it. Jacob continued to manipulate situations to his own advantage. Like his relatives, he needed a change of heart, but that probably never crossed their minds, and if it did, other thoughts overrode it. Situations deteriorated – heated up, and one day, it reached the point where Jacob became man on the run again. It was his transition time. He met and attempted to wrestle with God, and lost. That same loss, however was his gain. That encounter helped to establish him on a new path.

- Do you sometimes feel that someone's behavior has affected you? Or is it your own choices that have produced consequences? Discuss
- With whom do you relate in this story: Jacob or Esau?
- Why do you relate with your choice?

CHAPTER 3

Joseph: Dangerous dreaming

Joseph is one of the few Old Testament characters whose behavior was almost above reproach, and apart from Jesus who suffered more than anyone else ever has, or ever will, Joseph is probably the only other young person who suffered the atrocities he experienced, beginning at the hands of his own relatives. It does not mean that he did not have any faults. In fact, Scripture exposes the fact that he brought evil reports about his brothers, thus some have dubbed him a tattler. But even if that was the case, it pales in comparison to what he suffered. That aside however, God had a purpose, and although the process included harshness, it was nonetheless, a necessity.

He was next to the youngest of Jacob's twelve sons. His father, it seems, either failed to learn, or chose to ignore lessons from his parents' mistake of practicing favoritism. Joseph was his favorite, and that put the older sons' noses out of joint. Add to that, Joseph's knack for dreaming, and we see a pressure cooker waiting to explode – a Toro seeing red – a situation that spiralled out of control. After Joseph divulged two particular dreams, the older brothers' chagrin imploded. Disdain and envy occluded any flow of affection for their coddled, younger brother.

"Can you believe it? Who's the eldest here anyway?"

"The upstart. Such impudence and arrogance."

"Have a heart, brothers. He did not have his own mother to cuddle him and teach him manners."

"That's no excuse. Ben did not either, yet he does not behave with such impudence."

"The little raca. Let him dream on."

Even Jacob showed his displeasure: "Shall your mother, your brothers, and I pay obeisance to you Joseph? This is going too far." He however wondered about the dreams. It requires much effort to stifle dreams. Joseph could not control his. He did not ask for them, and he could not stop them. He described them, the way he saw them. He did not embellish them. His dreams would lead to a nightmare. That knack for dreams would actually lead to situations which surpassed any nightmare he or others could ever imagine.

Just like no one really intends to create problems, Jacob had no intention to spoil his home, and much less so, to aggrieve his older sons, yet that is what happened. To Jacob and Joseph, the coat represented love, but to the older sons: "You do not mean as much as Joseph does. He is something you're not, so he gets a token." Thus, a gesture which meant only goodwill, perpetuated a relationship which was already without any warmth and goodwill on the brother's side. Whenever they looked at Joseph they were like the bull seeing red. They wanted to run and charge, but they could not. Their dislike for him, and their silent fury over Jacob's action often bordered on charging ahead. They snorted and paced like the bull, and bided their time, waiting for the moment.

One day the opportunity presented itself without much scheming on their parts.

"Joseph" his father summoned.

"Here I am, Abba", he came running.

"Your brothers are in Schechem. They have much to do, and have no time to take a break, and eat well. Take this provision to them, right away."

"I will Abba."

Joseph was unaware he'd circled the area a few times. All the spots were cropped. The place was a maze. Which way should he take? The packages' weight was not a problem for a seventeen –year-old, but he longed to put them down. "Where do you want to go?" a man asked with concern, after he'd watched him circling several times.

"I am taking provisions to my brothers, the shepherds, sons of Jacob."

"The last time I saw them, they were headed that way", he indicated.

The brothers watched as the apparition became a body. It was Joseph! Red flag! The bull narrowed its eyes, lowered its head, snorted, paced and got ready to charge. As Joseph got closer, the particle in the pressure cooker lodged in the vent and .... Adrenaline laced with dislike, propelled muscles into action. What an opportunity! "Here comes that dreamer", one of them said, and all eyes and minds were on Joseph for the moment. He became the center of attraction for evil intentions.

The darkness of their silence descended upon Joseph and his stomach lurched. They're so quiet, he mused. His steps slowed. Maybe they are angry because they are hungry. After all, I lost time when I lost my way. I had better devise some means of remembering places. I must apologize also, and I'd better hurry up, he thought. However, he did not apologize. He could not, because he did not have the opportunity. Hey Yudah … Why? Asher? Of all my brothers, you …... Dan, please don't …. Gad what's the deal? His brothers seized the opportunity, and, grabbed Joseph. Some of them intended to get rid of the object of their pain – put an end to the dreamer and his dreams. Joseph also happened to be wearing *the* coat, a proof of their father's unfairness, as far as they were concerned. He was in their hands – at their disposal. Some of them did not want any bloodshed, but were still in cahoots with teaching him a lesson.

Thus, his nightmare began when they grabbed him, and stripped his gift from him. That must have hurt, because of the sentiment attached to it, but his nightmare worsened when they stole his identity, by selling him as a slave, into another culture. The people group who bought him were actually relatives, but ones with whom they no affinity, and as such, no interaction.

From a human perspective, Joseph's situation holds no attraction, rather it is something anyone would avoid. He suffered much more than anyone can imagine, and at the hands of those, whom both he and others would expect to protect him, instead of instigating the problems and difficulties he experienced. Identity theft is a devastating crime today. Joseph's own brothers stole his, and attempted to kill his dreams. His dreams, however, were just in detour.

Check out his account for yourself in Genesis 37, 39-45

- How can you identify with Joseph?
- How does it help you to change your mind?

CHAPTER 4

Moses: Right intention, wrong move

Apart from Jesus, many consider Moses the man who epitomizes meekness. But contrary to popular thought; meekness is not timidity, nor is it weakness. Looking at his life, it is clear that Moses was no weakling. On the contrary, he exhibited courage and faith. In fact, Scripture gives him accolades for his stance. It took much courage to identify with his people at that time. He had to live in two different worlds – the world that oppressed his people, and the Hebrew world, where his people were under oppression. He had a different – a peculiar background – different from anyone else's. Given his peoples' status, and the circumstances surrounding his birth, Moses was born into trouble, just like all of us. However, his were not a common occurrence.

There is no comparison with Jesus, but for the sake of argument, Moses had something in common with Jesus. The ruler, at the time of Jesus' birth legislated infanticide for all male babies a particular age. At Moses' birth, the ruler commanded infanticide for all Hebrew males during birth. Jesus' parents had to flee to Egypt to save their child. Moses' parents had to hide him to keep him alive, and they hid him on a river. What an unlikely place to hide something, let alone a baby. Water can soak and destroy things. Things can also sink in water. From a human perspective, his rescue and salvation have a twist, albeit positive, in a covert way.

Through adoption, he became the grandson of the same man who ordered the death of all Hebrew males at birth. Situations got more interesting when his adoptive mother hired his birth mother as his nurse, or nanny. There is no doubt that Jochebed his mother, told him stories which stirred passions in his heart. Yet he had to suppress them – put a leash on them, like keeping a leash on a puppy filled with energy and exuberance.

Liberty permits us to imagine that Moses at some point, experienced identity crises. Conditions which today, would elicit public outcry, scarred his childhood and his memories. He had dual nationality: A Hebrew by birth, an Egyptian through adoption. He could have boasted nobility, and isolate himself, instead he experienced unease. He knew that evil and ignorance dictated his people's circumstances. He seemed to be siding with the enemy, and he ached to help, but his hands were tied. However, scripture praises him for his desire to take sides with his people, rather than being counted as one of the privileged, one of those who oppressed his people. In the midst of all this, Moses however, like the rest of us, was not without faults.

Alongside his unfortunate circumstances, he had shortcomings. Anger management and manipulation of situations stood out. He later exhibited his inability to manage anger when he hit, rather than speak to the rock like God had instructed. That came with a cost. He also liked to rescue – to deliver, and there is nothing wrong with that, except when we take matters into our hands – manipulate situations. He had great intentions, and meant well but like the popular truism states: 'The way to destruction is often paved with good intentions.' He discovered that, and probably learned that some people misinterpret even well intentioned acts, and others will show no appreciation at all.

As he matured, his desire to help was like an itch in a spot which the fingers cannot access. He'd watched and internalised the situation with his people, and ached to do something to deliver them. The situation and his feelings created wounds which festered in his heart. He learned to practice restraint, but it was a task, and one day he lost that will to restrain his anger in that area. *Whop*, he heard, and upon examination, there was no blow for blow – no retaliation. *Whop*, another *whop*, and another. Still no retaliation, no effort at self-defence. He looked closer, and his sense of justice mingled with anger, and boiled. A Hebrew was receiving a battering. His rubber band of restraint snapped. Time to seize the opportunity. There was his chance to right at least one of the many wrongs. He would show that bully!

All the feelings of injustice, powerlessness and anger that had been festering, erupted. This is too much. I cannot let him kill the Hebrew, Moses probably rationalized. I cannot, and will not allow this to go on. He took the law into his own hands, and soon that offender would no longer abuse another Hebrew. It seemed he had no qualms about his action, until we see him running. He realized that something was wrong – actually much was wrong. He'd taken a life albeit, the life he took had abused someone else.

That tendency toward deliverance backfired one day. Wrestle, whop. He looked closer and sized up the situation. Similar scene. Different mood. Each party returned blows, but he could spot the aggressor –the bully. These Hebrews are trying to throttle each other. It seems their misunderstanding has progressed to the point of physical combat, and at the rate they are going, one of them will soon force the other out of this life. I must try to deescalate them. "Come on, break it up. You are brothers. Why are you trying to throttle each other?" he asked the instigator as he stood between them, probably waiting for the desired de-escalation. The fire of zeal in his heart fizzed out from the cold water of ingratitude and rejection thrown at it.

"Who made you a ruler over us? (Mind your own business) Are you trying to kill us like you did the Egyptian?", the bully spat, between breaths.

It was his business, but his approach was not timely. Moses liked neither the rebuff, nor the taste of fear, and he had received a cup of each. The questions were loaded, and the messages behind them demanded quick thinking and a plan. He realized that his status in the Pharaoh's family would not exempt him from his retribution. He therefore had no other option but escape, and once again he manipulated situations and fled. Moses was a man on the run. He became a shepherd in a neighboring country, until God used a spectacular sign to get his attention, and propel him into the task he had for him.

- Have you ever, and do you still claim justification in taking certain actions? Discuss.
- How does Moses' story so far, affect you?
- How can you begin to make changes – adjust some feelings?

CHAPTER 5

Hannah: The Tear-soaked years

Have you ever wanted something – longed for it to the extent where your failure or inability to obtain it, causes you, yourself to wonder about your logic? Hannah experienced that. She exhibited that behavior when she was sure she could not take it anymore. How she longed to have a child, if only for the sake of decreasing her rival's taunts. She however, had two strikes against her. One: she was a co-wife, and although it was a common practice then, there must have been times when she wished it was otherwise. But her wishes were akin to going around in a circle: she always ended up in the same place where she began – she could do nothing about the situation.

The second strike probably topped the list. Hannah could not have children, and the pain of barrenness obscured the fact that her husband loved her more than he loved Peninnah, the co-wife who had children. The secret and greater part of her pain, however, was the reality that God's hand was in it. "God had closed her womb." She knew that Elkanah loved her, but that was not enough to dilute the sting of her rival's taunts. The subculture did not offer any encouragement either. A great percentage of a woman's worth lay in her ability to bear children.

"Where are your children Hannah? When are you going to prove your worth?"

Every month she willed her the linings of her womb not to shed. She hoped – ached for those changes – signs and symptoms which would confirm pregnancy. Disappointment became like an X-ray jacket which the technician forgot to remove, and it was buttoned at the back where she could not access the opening to remove it. It oppressed and ravaged her mind, it soon wore her down, and subsequently it became a preoccupation, obscuring her perspective. Negativity and sorrow began to accumulate. One could say, Hannah had an obsession with becoming pregnant.

Her tears always flowed, although most of it was hidden. But one day she broke down and they spilled over, and became like a faucet that needed a new washer, and that washer was pregnancy. She wore her sorrow like a part of her clothing, while her appetite bordered on anorexia. Her husband noticed, but he did not seem to understand. How could he understand? Indeed, how could he ask such questions": "Why do you weep? Why don't you eat? Why is your heart grieved? Am I not better to you than ten sons?"

A light came on, something shifted in her heart as she considered the last question especially: 'Am I not better to you than ten sons?' The new bulb allowed the light to shine with greater effectiveness. She had much to think about: Wait a minute. He does understand. He is thinking about my situation. The words kindled a spark of hope, and she fanned it like someone hoping to get enough fire to heat a cold room. She dared to entertain the thought that maybe —maybe that bud of hope would bloom into reality.

Wouldn't it be something if I had ten sons? She grinned, gazing at the dream. But reality, like a gust of wind, knocked her dream over, shattering it. Her sigh rattled her frame. Okay, even one would be enough, and preferably a son. It would remove the venom from the sting in my rival's taunts. Her demeanor changed again for a moment as the realization spread right through her heart like a blanket enveloping, and spreading warmth throughout a cold body. Elkanah loved her, he'd proved it over and over, and she loved him. My behavior lacks fairness and rationality. Although my husband is a good man, he is not Yahweh after all. He has done his part. The problem is with me. He can sire children. Oh that Yahweh would open my womb. Her frame shook with her sigh. That realization has no pleasure. Yahweh has closed my womb.

Circumstances did not deter her from going to the temple and communicating with Yahweh. She continued to attend with steadfastness, and one day, when the meal was finished (hers picked at) she rose, prayed, and made a vow with a mixture of faith and desperation. She was still experiencing bitterness of soul. It was there like the scar tissue from a burn. Sighing and sorrowing marked each day, and were no less that day. Hannah poured out her request in silence, from a heart marinated in tears.

Eli her spiritual guide, not understanding her at the time she needed it, drew the wrong conclusion in rebuking her: "How much longer will you give in to drunkenness? Put away your wine". He was only doing his job, but he hurt rather than help her. She knew she was not above it, yet she knew she would never give in to that temptation. The account of Noah's inebriation and his denunciation of one of his sons, was like a watchdog. Still the accusation did not describe her behavior; neither did it define who she was. It stung like a scorpion, threatening to perpetuate her pain, but something had happened in her heart. It was minute, but real, and she recovered enough to respond, and she exercised caution, and maintained due respect, even as she corrected his false conclusion about her.

"No I am not drunk (*with wine, but with sorrow*) Do not consider me wicked. I am a woman of sorrow who has poured out her heart before the Lord." Her response awakened something in Eli, and he altered his attitude toward her, and even encouraged her: "May God grant you your request."

Her demeanor registered the change. She exchanged sorrow for joy. She aborted a sense of failure for faith. "The woman went her way and ate and her face was no longer sad." But she was human, and was not above sensitivity. The misconception was of importance and she wanted clearance: "Please let me find favor in your sight." She also asked a favor, and made a promise to God. She decided to believe that He heard her, and she acted like she believed that he had answered.

- Does Hannah's story make a difference?
- If it does, how does it affect your attitude so far? Discuss

CHAPTER 6

Naomi: A woman who digested bitterness

Naomi. Her parents had probably chosen that name with a purpose: refreshment against the backdrop of a time when unpleasantness abounded in the Hebrews' lives. She grew up in a time marred by civil war and other uncertainties. She recalled her parents frequently bewailing the time when their people ceased to obey and honor Yahweh, and as a result, many of the local leaders often wore sack-cloth, and poured ashes over their skin. Her tribe tried to follow Yahweh's edicts, not that anyone was without blame. She was then married, and had two sons.

Elimelech her husband, talked about relocating and she was not keen about it, but his word was law. She was a woman, thus she had nothing of significance to say in the matter. Furthermore, their circumstance justified the move. After all, they were in the midst of a famine, and maybe the move would prevent starvation. Besides, she loved and trusted her husband; a man who worshipped and honored Yahweh at a time when judges ruled, and many 'did what was right in his own eyes.' Naomi was aware that Yahweh had blessed her. She was complete. She had all that she could desire in her family of four, including their two boys. She, however, nursed doubts and fears, and wondered how they would fare. She hoped there'd be no more tragedies.

She'd heard it often, and was familiar with the stories filled with tragedy and sorrow. One tribe, the Benjamites was almost decimated, due to some evil they'd committed. They'd shown disdain for Yahweh and His ways. Following the decimation, there were not enough females for matrimony. Some from the other tribes grieved for them, recalling a vow which they could not revoke, and therefore, offered the best advice they could. Subsequently, the Benjamite men had to use force – kidnap women from another tribe, to marry and replenish their diminished tribe.

The day arrived. Naomi and her family became economic migrants. She assumed that everyone had the same mindset. She had learned that her people should never turn away foreigners, based on the fact that they themselves were once aliens in a foreign land. She'd discussed the topic with Elimelech, because like him, she'd heard the story about Joshua, one of their leaders with an impressive military portfolio. Yet, a group of people who pretended that they were destitute travellers, deceived him. Anyhow, one incentive finally pushed them into Moab: they had children to feed. And despite the fact that it was not far away, it was still a strange culture and, she'd overheard respected leaders and teachers who feared Yahweh, discourage any intimate communion with the people whose land they were entering. She wondered how they would fare.

Over time, they settled into life in their new country and were there for ten years. During that time however, sorrow struck, as death dwindled her family when her beloved Elimelech 'went the way of all the earth' – 'was gathered to his fathers.' Then her sons married, and the two occasions took her mind off her sorrow for a while. But sorrow struck again when her older son Mahlon, 'rested with his father (s)', and while the fire of that grief still smouldered in her heart, her other son 'rested with his father and his brother.' Although it was reality, sometimes she still could not believe it.

Her men rested with their fathers during their sojourn. They'd arrived as a family of four, grew to six through marriage, had no off-springs, and were diminished to three – three women – all widows. Naomi was, by then, at the end of her wits, and didn't know what to do. A small glow –faith as small as fire from a struck match, penetrated and interrupted the tumult in her heart. She heard that God was revisiting His people in her homeland. It piqued her interest, reawakened hope, and she decided it was time to return home.

The three women started out to return together to Naomi's' land, but she dissuaded the young women from going with her. What do I have to show, much less to give them? Hasn't Yahweh taken away everything from me? The thoughts, like a bitter medicine, coursed through her. It would not work, she had to lay it out: "My daughters, it will be much better for you to return to your people. Who knows? Marriage may be a part of your future. May Yahweh grant that, and other blessings too." They behaved like many women do on such occasions, they spilled their hearts through their eyes.

Orpah picked sense out of nonsense – saw the logic in her mother-law's declaration, and decided to return to her people, but Ruth chose, actually vowed to stay with her. Naomi at that time, did not feel – actually for a long time, she had not felt anything close to 'pleasantness.' She tried not to wear it on her sleeves, but without success. She was going home, but was filled with emptiness. What was there for her, a widow, and to make matters worse, one without off-springs? She had nothing but grief to show for the ten years of sojourn away from her homeland.

Her heart felt like lead, and it was as though wormwood mingled with blood and circulated through her. All this, despite the fact that a daughter-in law, full of sensitivity, love and dedication, had volunteered, and was now her companion. Naomi wore dejection, and was so focused on her grief, that she did not even take note of the fact that when she left years ago, famine was rife, but she was returning at Barley harvest. She and her daughter-in-law caused quite a stir, and when some former acquaintances inquired whether or not it was Naomi whom they were looking at, she rejected her name, and requested, "Call me Bitter, because the Almighty has afflicted me. I went away full, and returned empty." The heart's content spills out during times of testing, and Naomi's did as she arrived at her wit's end.

- Maybe you're at your wits' end. How does Naomi's heart leak affect you at this stage?

God likes to meet people where they are, especially at their wit's end. Maybe this poem will encourage you.

Are You at Wits End Corner?

Are you standing at "Wits End Corner" Christian, with troubled brow'
Are you thinking of what is before you, and all you are bearing now'
Does all the world seem against you, and you in the battle alone'
Remember at Wits End Corner Is where God's power is shown.

Are you standing at "Wits End Corner" Blinded with wearying pain
Feeling you cannot endure it, you cannot bear the strain.
Bruised through the constant suffering Dizzy and dazed, and numb
Remember at Wits End Corner, is where Jesus loves to come

Are you standing at "Wits End Corner" Your work before you spread?
Or lying begun, unfinished and pressing on heart and head.
Longing for strength to do it. Stretching out trembling hands
Remember at "Wits End Corner" The burden bearer stands.

Are you standing at "Wits End Corner" Yearning for those you love,
Longing and praying and watching, pleading their cause above,
Trying to lead them to Jesus Wondering if you've been true'
He whispers at "Wits End Corner" "I'll win them as I won you?"

Are you standing at "Wits End Corner" Then you're just in the very
spot.
To learn the wondrous resources of Him who fails not!
No doubt to a brighter pathway your footsteps will soon be moved
But only at Wits End Corner Is the God who is able, "proved."[7]

CHAPTER 7

Ruth: A widow, a foreigner, a gleaner

She often wished they (the women) would sometimes remove their veils, and look fully into each other's faces, and see the persons behind them. The veils seemed to do more than hide faces: they hid expressions, and stifled spontaneity. What do they really think of me? She sometimes worried. She was not unaware of two facts: she was from a despised people, and she was only a female gleaner. This was her first full year, actually a little over a year since she entered her new country, culture, and new life. Her mind scrolled back to some early scenes.

During the adjustment period, she'd requested permission to help her mother-in-law. Naomi was okay with the request, and Ruth started to glean after Naomi warned her to practice caution because the position posed various risks. Ruth followed instructions, and was finding gleaning an occupation filed with interest and surprises. One day, the owner Boaz himself, greeted, encouraged, and instructed her about her task.

She loved her mother-in-law Naomi, and she knew Naomi loved her too. 'My daughter', she addressed her. The thought elicited a smile, and memories rushed her heart, kidnapping her to a not-too distant past. 'Wherever you go, I will go. Your people shall be my people, and your God, my God. "I will never you", she'd vowed. She was never sorry that she made that decision.

She recalled the time they entered her country – a family of four, with two sons. There was talk about famine in the land where they came from. Their arrival had also re-awakened and stimulated rumours. One point they discussed was the fact that they were related to her people, but it seemed no one had the courage, or the willingness to disclose and discuss the reason (s) for the segregation. There were others migrants like them, but that family stood out.

Their ways were different, and provoked many behind-doors, and over-the-wall, cautious discussions. Some reported that they claimed that Yahweh, the creator dealt intimately with them. Before long, they gained respect and acceptance, but sorrow soon visited the family. Elimelech died – "Was gathered to his fathers, but the Yahweh is with His people", the solemn prophet remarked. It seemed like death in the family swung peoples' hearts door wider to understanding and accepting the family. Ruth herself had swallowed and assimilated some of those words the prophet exclaimed. More – harsh memories resurfaced as she recalled the myrrh -embalmed, swaddling cloth- wrapped body, laid in the side of the earth. The women in the village noticed, and had talked about the change in Naomi. It was as though she had lost a part of herself, she had swallowed sorrow, and it inebriated her.

The focus had soon shifted for a while, however. Mahlon the older son, and Orpah were pledged to each other in marriage, and the wedding including all the details, helped to dilute some of the sorrow, as Naomi, no doubt, dreamed of descendants. Not long after that, Chillion the younger son asked for Ruth's hand in marriage. Ruth liked Naomi her to-be mother-in-law, and counted it a pleasure to contribute to her hope and happiness.

Ruth's smile widened as she recalled that particular scene, and she was particularly thankful that her veil hid her face that day her father summoned her to his presence, notified her about the request, and pronounced his endorsement. Under the cover of the veil, she was grinning. She had for a long time, admired, loved, and dared to dream about the soft-spoken, generous stranger dwelling among them. She'd nevertheless followed protocol, and with expected shyness, accepted the offer. The wedding nuptial was worth remembering. What a time of celebration and happiness.

Despite the heat of the day, she shivered, and a sigh escaped as a dark cloud overshadowed the horizon of pleasant memories. Their union had produced no offspring, and the likelihood of her remarrying and bearing any, was now non-existent. The only one who by law, could actualize that possibility, was himself deceased – like his brother.

Her busy hands slackened as the memories continued, and she lost her sense of time and place, as she gazed into the past.

She'd grieved for Naomi upon Elimelech's passing, then joy visited for a while with Mahlon's marriage, and shortly after that, Chillion's. Sorrow however, revisited them – burst in upon them. That time it was Oprah's turn to drink that cup, and how Ruth grieved once again for Naomi, because that was her second cup. Mahlon was "resting with his fathers", as the solemn prophet once again, encouraged. Ruth now realized that trials are a part of life's tapestry. She nevertheless, wished that she could receive hints about their arrival so that she could get prepared. But although she'd learned that she should expect them, they still took her by surprise. Her hand rested, with immobility over an ear of corn. It had been like a déjà vu – a double déjà vu.

She'd wished she would wake up and realize it was only a bad dream, but the activities: family, relatives, and friends coming by in silent streams, Flutists playing dirges, Naomi not looking half like herself, and neighborhood children with wide, solemn, questioning eyes watching everything, proved it was worse than a nightmare. It had been her turn to drink the cup, and it was bitter. But again, she'd thought of Naomi who had to drink it three times. Yet another myrrh-drenched, swaddling-cloth covered body was laid in the side of the earth, close to the previous two. Chillion was resting with his father and brother, but in her heart, she resented it, she did not want that – not yet. But like all others, she had no control over reality, and especially death. Life moved on, and Naomi one day divulged that she'd decided to return to her home-land. Both Ruth and Oprah wanted to go with her, but Oprah went back to her people after Naomi in her jocularity, painted a graphic word picture.

Ruth smiled despite the pain, as she recalled Naomi looking them in the eyes, and saying: "Go home my daughters. Even if I remarry, and bear sons, surely you would not wait around for them to reach marriageable age and marry them, would you?" Oprah saw a reality she did not like, and changed her mind, but Ruth knew she would not – could not leave her mother-in-law. Their relationship was like a knitted garment. She could not leave her mother-in-law, any more than she could unravel a single strand from one part of the garment, without affecting the whole. Thus she had vowed not to leave her.

She'd settled down, and learned to love her new people, although sometimes she was not sure of their love for her. She especially loved the way friends encouraged Naomi, but now it was over a year, and she could see Naomi's increasing concern for her. She wished she could prevent her from worrying, for even though Naomi admitted that situations had improved, it was still difficult for two widows living together. She snapped to attention as someone snickered and said: 'There goes that foreigner, dreaming again.'

Where am I? She glanced about her. Two women, while they worked, glanced her way. One of them shook her head, and with a voice filled with warmth, concern and kindness; remarked: "My sister, you dream on your feet. Dreams belong to the night, upon your bed. Glean while you can. If you continue to dream, you will glean only the wind, and that will not fill empty stomachs. Besides, this job is filled with danger. Why don't you wait until you complete your tasks?"

Ruth smiled her thanks, bowing slightly, grateful that her veil hid her tears of gratitude. The words' undertones warmed her heart and quickened her muscles. As the wind wafted the spikenard's fragrance her way, she let the same wind drive her worries away like chaff. She checked her basket. It was almost full of various grains. She and Naomi would later sort and prepare them; and make meals which would nourish them, and anyone else who needed feeding. The anticipation of that coming interaction lightened her heart even more.

- If you do, how do you relate to Ruth's story?

CHAPTER 8

Post Breaking Points

"Before I was afflicted I went astray, but now I keep your word."[8]

When a parent takes a naughty child to task, or when a teacher disciplines – challenges students in order to stimulate improvement, it is only for a while. Although not all (little) offenders show repentance, nor all students accept and appreciate discipline, yet it's a necessity. Teachers and parents especially, know however, that prolonged separation and any disciplinary measures can over time, ruin the spirit, more than it corrects a misbehaviour, or improve attitude.

God acts in like manner toward His children. Even when sin is not a part of the situation, He allows trials, and He disciplines His children for good reasons, and for a season. Listen to His heart: "I will not contend forever, nor will I always be angry; for the spirit would fail before me, and the souls which I have made."[9]

Each of the noted characters was different –worlds apart. Era, age, gender, profession, station and status, are only a few of the differences. Yet they had one thing in common. They all experienced crises which at the time made so sense, and seemed to have no solution. They did not understand what was happening, nor did they know why. Some of them probably did not even think about it. We, however from this side, see what they did not. Even where sin was not in the picture, God orchestrated situations, and stretched his people. The gems in rough, needed polishing. Whether it was correction or just discipline, station and status did not set them apart.

Jewellers remark: "Most gems look dull, so they are polished to look smooth and shiny. They are cut to shape to make them sparkle." [10] Sounds similar to what God does through the trials He allows. God prepared them for the tasks he had, lined up for them. Listen to the hearts of the mentioned characters, after their breaking points.

CHAPTER 9

Jacob: From a self-made man, to Patriarch of God's chosen people

Just like some people with heart problems need a heart transplant in order to survive, so we all need a new, a transformed heart, and Jacob was someone who needed that. He had several incidents which should have shaken him up, or rather should have caused him to reconsider his ways, but it seems that it was after only after meeting and wrestling with God, then limping away from his presence, that he arrived at the necessary breaking point in his life.

At that stage, he teetered at the precipice of distress, and although there were still some rough edges, maturity was settling in. He had gone through the fire (some of which was his own making) especially when he deceived Esau, then ran away to live with relatives. However, the refining fire started when Laban deceived him by giving him the wrong wife. But because he loved Rachel, he was willing to work extra years for her. Coupled with that problem, were forced polygamy including surrogate mothering, co-wife competition and squabbling, and the time when he had to rebuke his beloved Rachel who could not have children, and pestered him to the point of anger. In addition to those problems, his uncle changed his wages three times. But Jacob dealt in an underhanded way too. He had an ongoing problem: he knew how to get what he wanted.

Mandrakes dotted the hillsides, and their headiness and significance lifted his sandal-height spirits. He had a shepherd's heart, and missed nothing. Their value was a recent discovery. The ewe that grazed close to the mandrake bushes seemed to calve with more ease and, in abundance. An idea grew and flourished, became a dream, and then a plan. His plan flourished as long as no one got wind about it. It seemed, however, that trouble knew where to find him. Before long, his relatives began to complain and make insinuations which bordered on accusation.

Situations heated up like the mid-day sun in the Sahara. His tolerance level dropped, and Jacob jumped out of the fire – became man on the run again, but this time with responsibilities, and thus, burdens. After going a short distance, he was in for a surprise (although he should not have been) when Laban, filled with indignation, caught up with him, lectured him, and worst of all, accused him of stealing their household gods! (He did not know that his beloved Rachel had taken them) Jacob, however, was not mealy mouthed. He confronted Laban about some of his unfair dealings which had driven him to take matters into his own hands – manipulate situations.

After making an emotionally-charged covenant, they parted ways, and fatigue set in, especially at the thought of meeting with his twin, whom he'd gypped as a young man. Once again, Jacob tried to manipulate situations in his schemes to get around his impending unpleasantness. While he anticipated that meeting, he met some angels, and realized that God wanted to be a part of his life. The meeting with this brother passed without much stress, and Jacob must have been breathed gratitude and relief that none of the horrors he anticipated, including his schemes to appease his brother, were necessary.

Following the confrontations, Jacob just wanted to be alone, so that he could think, and while he was alone, he experienced a Theophinine. A man wrestled with him till close to daybreak. He eventually threw Jacob's hip out of joint, and gave him a new name. Jacob limped away, but with a name that bore much significance, and the beginning of a new heart – mindset. We see his life from our point in history, and the changes seems small. Like we do sometimes, Jacob slipped up. Nonetheless there were changes. Some of those changes are evident in Joseph's character. Disappointment and sorrow over the fact that all his sons did not internalize and portrayed his good teaching is legitimate, but it is obvious that he tried to teach and instill in them, the ways of Yahweh. Like some of us, (and I speak for myself) Jacob was a slow learner. He still had much to learn.

He would experience much grief, due to three of his sons' behavior. In the heat of a seemingly justifiable revenge, they killed the men of a village, after one of their number raped Dinah, their sister. Jacob's reaction showed that he still lacked maturity in some areas, but he had matured enough to know that the manner in which they handled the situation was wrong. Later on, some of his older sons, after they'd sold Joseph, deceived Jacob into believing that he was dead (as far as they were concerned, he was dead to them) Jacob mourned and wept; and just knew that his grief would 'bring him to his grave'. However, he lived to learn that his son was alive, and he even went to live with him. He became the esteemed patriarch of the twelve tribes of Israel, from one of which Jesus would descend physically. Jacob had to experience all the hardships, so that he could receive the conditioning and honing, necessary for his role. Jacob had a change in outlook, and that took a long time. He also had a name change with much significance.

- What is it from your past: a name? or something else that evoke images? And what images?
- In Jacob's story, can you see any resemblance to any issue with which you struggle?

CHAPTER 10

Joseph: Beyond the wildest dream

When Joseph's brothers sold him, and the Ishmaelites took him away, he must have been at times, overwhelmed with a sense of helplessness and rejection. It was not until much later that he viewed his situation through the lens of faith. Until then, he could not figure out what was happening: Jacob sent him to take provisions to his brothers; and not only had he acted in obedience, he'd also complied with pleasure. The place was, however, like a maze, and he went around in circles until a man in kindness, showed him the way. As he'd approached them, he could not help noticing their silence, and it awakened unease in his heart. He'd however, calmed himself with his homemade philosophy, and had theorized that tiredness and hunger provoked their mood. All he had to do was apologize for his tardiness.

Memories, like scenes he did not relish, continued to parade across his mind. He recalled how he had no chance to apologize to his brothers, because some of them, he could not recall who, grabbed him, while others stripped off his favourite coat in anger. The horrors had continued. He was soon crouching in shock, in the dankness and darkness of a pit, overwhelmed with the fear that he would drown. I t was however empty, but before he had time to wonder about their behavior; they pulled him out, and the next thing he recalled, was a group of people in a caravan, taking him away. He was up to that point, sure his father would soon come to deliver him, but that did not happen. The next thing he recalled, was strangers looking him over, then he landed in a new country.

Why does Abba not come to take me home? Why did my brothers express anger? Why did they throw me in the cistern? Why did Abba send me to them, if he knew they were angry? Was it a conspiracy? No. Abba loves me. He would never do that. He will surely come to rescue me.

He soon stopped hoping, but he had no time to worry. Busyness marked his days. He had many responsibilities, and his master showed him kindness. He recalled many truths and lessons his father taught him, and he tried to apply them. Joseph learned to trust God without any boundaries. All seemed to be going well, considering his situation, but one thing was amiss. One day, he was preoccupied with is duties when his master's wife approached him. That was not the first time he became aware of some of the more delicate intricacies of life. The blood circulating in his veins thundered in his ears, and he tasted fear, and something else. He did not like what was happening. He did not like the way his master's wife behaved. Situations escalated, and finally, one day he had to escape from her presence.

I will not do this wicked thing. It would not honor Yahweh., and besides Abba said it is not the way to handle this situation.

He dashed from the room, and even when he realized he'd left his coat – hard evidence in her hand, he did not return for it. The next thing he knew, two men he recognized, approached, arrested, and put in him prison.

Why is this happening? Why am I here? I have done no wrong. Why does Yahweh allow this to happen? Why does He not deliver me? he probably despaired.

But while he was there, he looked out for others and their needs, and his knack for interpreting dreams would one day become his bail. He began by interpreting dreams for two fellow inmates.

"Why are you clothed in glumness? He asked an inmate whose eyes betrayed his heart.

"We both had dreams", he said, including another equally troubled looking inmate, "and there's no one to interpret them."

"Does not all interpretations belong to Yahweh? Tell me your dream", he invited.

"I had a dream too", the other inmate confided, after he watched the interaction.

His interpretations were correct and one of the inmates fared well, and was restored to his position. Demise was the outcome for the other. The one who experienced mercy made a promise which he forgot. Thus Joseph lingered longer in prison. But God had a plan and a purpose. The overseer too, had dreams which riddled his mind, and once again Joseph's knack with dreams helped him, and was his bail. That was after the man with the memory lapse suddenly remembered. Joseph soon stood before the overseer, listened to his dreams, and interpreted them with precision. It's hard to see God's hand in it, but Scripture declares: "Moreover, He (God) called for a famine in the land, He destroyed the provision of bread. He sent a man before them- Joseph- who was sold as a slave. They hurt his feet with fetters, he was laid in irons. Until the time that his word came to pass, God's word tested him, the king sent and released him, the ruler of the people let him go free. He made him lord of his house, and ruler of all his possessions, to bind his princes at his pleasure, and teach his elders wisdom."[11]

It cannot be more succinct. God's ways are past finding out. In the interim, Joseph received a new name: 'One who feeds.' He also married, and he sired two sons. His brothers saw what became of his dreams. Joseph showed his emotional side when he wept with joy over seeing his younger brother (Genesis 43: 29-31) He also wept when he finally revealed himself to his brothers, (Genesis 45:1-2) and when he saw his beloved father after many years. (Genesis 46:29) He also showed sternness, but it was only a front to test his brother's attitudes.

No one expects or even imagines a slave or prisoner experiencing ascendancy, and much less so, to the position Joseph assumed. Joseph later reassured his brothers: "You intended to harm me, but God intended it for good. He brought me to this position so I could save the lives of many." (Genesis 50:19-21)

Everyone's situation is different, and God does not necessarily work the same way in every case. He is, however aware, and is working out His own purpose, and His plan in everyone's life. He does not have to explain anything, and is aware of our humanness in our reactions. He offers equal measures of grace for everyone in every situation, regardless of the severity. He is willing to wait for us to learn His ways and cooperate with Him.

Throughout the entire ordeal, Joseph experienced a change of culture, perception, and name. He could not control the change of culture, nor the name change. His attitude, however had much to do with the change in perception – he learned through all he experienced. The boy who was sold into slavery, and was incarcerated despite his innocence, became overseer, and fed many like his name implies.

- Does this part of Joseph's story resonate with any issues with which you may be battling? If so, how can you resolve them in the light of this narrative?

CHAPTER 11

From shepherd, to God-appointed Deliverer

When Moses entered Midian, one of his first activities involved delivering – rescuing. He noticed some shepherds intimidating some young women, and he could not help it, he had to help them. That knack to rescue resurfaced, and that time his intervention produced positive returns. Jethro/Reuel the young women's father, offered him Zipporah as his wife.

Nevertheless, much was against him. Some of it he was aware of, and some he did not even think about. He must have yearned to see his adoptive family, as well as his blood relatives, but he dared not re-enter Egypt. What he did – killing the Egyptian was criminal, albeit justifiable, and could have cost him his life, as well as that of his own relatives, plus exacerbating the entire situation for the Hebrew people. Actually, when he killed the Egyptian, it was a show of self-help, although he viewed it then, as defending, helping his people. Fear propelled him to run, and he was not thinking about Yahweh then, he did not trust him to iron out the situation.

Over time, he must have become resigned to his situation: a run-away son of nobility, as well as a kind of refugee. His heart must have still ached for his people, but it is doubtful that he still entertained any thoughts about delivering, and much less, leading anyone. His sheep and his own family were his focus then. Life continued and he adapted himself as much as it was possible for him to do in his situation. The agrarian society valued sheep herding. It was a popular occupation, it was money, thus a livelihood

One day, as Moses tended his sheep, something caught his attention. A burning bush was not an unusual sight, but there was something different – spectacular about the one he was witnessing. Although it burned, it was not consumed. It piqued his interest, and aroused his curiosity. I must see this, he thought, and he tried to investigate the phenomena before him.

With his eyes fixed on the object of interest, he tried to approach but something else, something even more spectacular arrested his senses. He heard a voice, but saw no one.

"Moses!"

Am I hearing voices? Yahweh? How did he know my name?

"Do not come any closer. Remove your sandals, Moses. You are standing in a holy place."

Is this really happening? He wondered.

Yes, it was reality. God appeared to him and gave him a commission. In summary, He knew and cared about His peoples 'plight, and wanted to deliver them – lead them out of bondage, and Moses was the one for the task. But while Moses was glad about God's concern, and His proposed intervention, he felt no excitement nor keenness about his role in it. He did not think God had the right person, and he let him know it. The whole idea was so far-fetched to Moses, it provoked his stuttering. To prove that Yahweh was mistaken, he tried another line:

"I … I … have a pr …. oblem s … speaking. M y b bro ther A a ron would d d o better. Wh y n ot send him instead? Besides, my neck would be on the block, because it is a certainty that the new Potiphar learned what happened years ago when I was a younger man, he thought.

"Who made man's mouth, Moses?"

He knew he had lost the argument. God would not back down. Moses was on his way to Egypt and beyond.

What contradictions. How far removed Moses' thoughts were from God's at that time. It is a fact that His ways are far above ours, yet we can learn from His ways. Initially, Moses was not ready for God's commission. When he tried to help as a younger man, he was neither fit nor ready, and when God knew he was, Moses did not think he was the right person for the job. God had however, through Moses's tasks as a shepherd, prepared him to lead, and take care of His sometimes, wayward people. The burning bush was his way of getting his attention, so he could propel him into his task as leader through the wilderness. And by the time he started (a point which reassures me personally) his new assignment, he was eighty years old!

Nothing about Moses came anywhere close to perfection. Later, while he led the people, his inability to control his anger cost him the privilege of leading his people to the promised land. Nevertheless, God refers to him as 'my servant', and he 'conversed with God as a man talks with his friend.' Moreover, Moses learned to trust the great I AM. "Tell them I AM sent you." Like one speaker puts it: "Faith replaces fear when we focus on God's character."[12]

Moses learned to do that. He believed, replaced his fears with faith, and dared to return to Egypt and face some of those fears.

Read all about it in Exodus

- If you can, in what ways can you relate to Moses?

CHAPTER 12

Hannah: From tear soaked years to a joyful mother of a prophet and more.

"He makes all things beautiful in His time." And "what God closes, no man open." Likewise, what He opens, no man can close." These facts describe Hannah's case. Her tear soaked years soon ended. After her heartfelt request and her interaction with Eli, she left the temple with a new mindset. "She ate, and her face was no longer sad." God knew her heart, and would work out His plan and purpose.

He'd seen her tears, and heard her heart's cry. He'd not forgotten, He'd just held His plans in check until His appointed time, then He'd opened Hannah's womb, and she was pregnant at last. When Samuel her gift was born, she gave him back - loaned him to God. When she weaned him, she brought him to the temple, and from a tender age, Samuel became Eli's disciple. It must have been with difficulty that she sometimes thought of giving up the baby for whom she'd wept, prayed, and waited. Yet she loaned him to God.

Tragedy and sorrow marked that time in her people's history. Many had chosen to disregard God's ways, so messages from Him were rare, and visions were not a common occurrence. God, however, interacted with the young Samuel, and chose him to deliver to the nation, a message that did not offer any pleasure. He became a great leader and prophet. The people revered him, recognizing God's power upon him. He anointed Israel's first king (at their insistence) and later, God's appointed king: King David.

Hannah knew and worshipped Yahweh. She owned her feelings, and was not timid about her humanness. She cried and she rejoiced. she had questions, some of which she voiced. Her once sad heart became like a fountain that spewed out praise, as she acknowledged Yahweh's sovereignty. "The Lord kills and makes alive, He brings down to the grave and brings up. He brings low and lifts up",[13] she acknowledged and avowed. Hannah had other children after Samuel: three sons and two daughters, and was a joyful and a grateful mother.

Hannah experienced a change in her outlook. At the start of the story we saw her weeping, and at the close, she glorified God. See her story in First Samuel.

- How does Hannah's story at this point influence you to view your particular circumstances?

CHAPTER 13

Naomi: Pleasantness restored

Naomi may have lost focus for a while, but she knew and owned her feelings, although they lacked consistency with Yahweh's thoughts toward her. She recognized his sovereignty. Maybe like some of us, for a while, she confused priority with urgency. She considered her family her completeness and in her depths of grief when they died, she perceived her loss as "Jehovah's affliction of her soul." She however, admitted that she had bitterness and in the process, risked vulnerability through her confession.

Nevertheless, throughout her ordeal, that hidden, pleasant side for which she is named, peeked through like a strand of sunshine, through dark clouds. She was a woman who had much love. It is first of all evident in her grief for her husband and sons. She also loved Yahweh, and had faith enough to desire to be a part of his visitation upon His people. Her love is also evident in her feelings toward her daughters-in-law. When she dissuaded them from accompanying her, she was only showing her concern for their welfare, although some pride leaked.

She desired and longed to see situations flow according the law regarding redemption. She knew, and embraced the recommendation, that if a married man died and had no children, then his brother would marry that widow, so that he could carry on his brother's name. It grieved her soul that she could not contribute to carrying on her husband's name. Her love is also evident in her growing concern for her daughter-in-law, when she lived with her. Her gradual, revived faith gave her insight into possibilities not evident to other eyes. Possibilities abounded.

Wasn't Boaz the owner? Better yet, wasn't he related to her departed husband? She was a matchmaker as well as an avid schemer at the same time. She gave Ruth etiquette lessons. The greater part of the lessons centered on how to get Boaz' attention – how to let him know that she was available and ready. Thus, she gathered information in a subtle way: "Where did you glean today?" That question was not as simple as it appeared. It was full of significance known only to her.

Friends lavished upon her, words of encouragement, and she thrived on them. She lived to dandle her first grandchild Obed, David's grandfather, on her knees. Her loss and heartache, prepared her for something new and bigger. It was as though God emptied her of everything she deemed important, in order to fill her up anew with something far beyond her expectation.

Naomi experienced changes in circumstances. (Read it for yourself in the book of Ruth) She had no control over situations like the famine and the loss of her family. Her reaction, however, was her responsibility, and had much significance. She wavered a little, but bounced back. The changes she experienced, and her response helped others, and can still influence others today.

- How does Naomi's story affect your outlook at this point?
- Could your perception use some adjustment?

CHAPTER 14

Ruth: From foreign gleaner to a mother in Israel

Ruth anticipated her mother-in-law's question: "Where did you glean today my daughter?" and the answer was usually related to Naomi's instructions. Ruth wondered why she asked that question, not knowing it was loaded. And that particular day, she'd felt an extra surge of happiness over the other gleaner's words, and the message they portrayed. She'd several times overheard some remarks regarding her status, but most of the others, were, however, good to her, and she'd followed Naomi's advice.

One day, Naomi gave her some strange advice, and although Ruth was probably a bit nervous, she loved and trusted her mother-in-law, so did not have to think twice about following her instructions. But later, her heart felt as though it would leap from her chest when Boaz demanded to know who she was. She followed Naomi's advice, and Boaz explained the situation, and made a proposal. He also gave her a measure of barley, his sign to Naomi that he understood, and was ready to honor his dead relative.

Following with steadfastness, the culture's protocol, Boaz, the kinsman redeemer, later married Ruth, and they became the progenitors of Israel's royal lines – kings. Ruth who was from a despised group, and was a foreign gleaner, and a childless widow, became the matriarch of kings, and specifically King David's great-grand-mother.

Ruth had no control over her changes, except her response and reaction. We see her heartwarming response to Naomi: "Do not ask me to leave you". Her response helped to change history. God may not necessarily do the same for another as He did for Ruth, but He has a plan for everyone, although the route each person takes, may be contrary to our preconceived idea of God: how we expect Him to behave, and what we think He should do.

- How do you expect God to act? Does He act in contradiction to your expectations?
- With which of these characters can you relate?
- If you can relate, how will you allow God to change your attitude?

CHAPTER 15

Horatio Spafford: Song from a wounded heart

Like many other Christians, I like and appreciate the song: "It is well with my soul." I have liked it since I heard it as a young girl, and from my human perspective, I used to imagine the author wrote it from a life full of peace and pastoral experiences. That was, however, not the case but rather, the extreme opposite. Horatio Spafford the author, wrote it under circumstances which came nowhere close to pleasantness. In fact, he and many like him, have spoken and written from the wounds and pain in their lives.

"Horatio was a lawyer with much prominence in the 1800s, but in the great fires of Chicago, he lost most of his investment. Later, after the stress of his loss, he decided to take a holiday in Europe, and sent his family ahead of him. While he was on route to join them, he received news of the ship's collision with another, and heart-wrenching fact that his four daughters were among those who'd perished. It was during that time that he penned the lyrics to 'It is well with my soul.'

The Spaffords eventually had more children, but tragedy struck again when their four-year-old son died. A few years later", however, the couple drank their sorrow and got up again. Along with others, they went to Jerusalem and helped establish the American Colony – a charitable agency."[14]

Although we mean well when we seek to offer comfort to those who grieve, only those who have experienced the same depth of grief can understand. The Spaffords had their share, actually more than their share of grief that must squeezed and wounded their hearts. Sorrow was an ingredient among the many emotions, yet a song – and one which has inspired and challenged many to bear their cross – leaked from his wounded heart. They had learned like Paul did, to be content, if not glad, in every situation. The Spafford's proved that we often learn more from times of sorrow and loss, than we do when all is going well – when all is going according to what we expect and desire.

1. When peace, like a river, attends my way,
   When sorrows like sea billows roll;
   Whatever my lot, you have taught me to say,
   It is well, it is well with my soul.

2. Though Satan should buffet, though trials should come,
   Let this blest assurance control,
   That Christ has regarded my helpless estate,
   and has shed His own blood for my soul.

Trials expose us, and just like a rose usually gives off its fragrance when bruised or crushed, trails extract the contents of our hearts. A speaker recently summed it up like this: "Blessings do not teach us as much as trials do."[15] "Trials are blessings clothed in pain", another song writer states. These are facts that I am learning. Our hearts, however, need to be in tune – aligned with God's ways. We need to guard our hearts, so that like the rose which gives a fragrance when crushed, we will give off the fragrance of Christ. "Keep your hearts with all diligence, for out of your hearts flow the issues of life",[16] God admonishes.

The Spaffords probably had no idea that their change in circumstances would be so far reaching. Yet it continues to bless and challenge many.

- What's in your heart?
- How does the Spaffords story affect of influence your thoughts?

CHAPTER 16

Fanny Crosby: Physical blindness, sharp, effective insight

Just like He did in the days of the Old Testament characters, and others, through later centuries, God continued right through the eighteenth century, to condition His people through hardships. Fanny Crosby was one of those who experienced such a conditioning. Her songs have blessed and inspired many Christians throughout the nineteenth century and beyond. No one knows her breaking point, but she had several situations which tested her faith. According to one source, she became blind when she was only six weeks old due to an illness. She did not know a father, because he died when she was one-year-old.

Life was difficult at the best of times. Her mother however, discouraged the poor me attitude. Fanny attended a school for the blind, and had a normal education, and childhood. Her grandmother was a great spiritual influence, and helped to ground her in God's word. Fanny was married, but their only child died in infancy. After the death of her child, she wrote the hymn, Safe in the arms of Jesus. Fanny was also an advocate for the visually impaired, and was instrumental in lobbying for schools for the blind.[17]

1. Safe in the arms of Jesus,
   Safe on His gentle breast;
   There by His love o'ershaded,
   sweetly my soul shall rest.
   Hark! 'Tis the voice of angels

Borne in a song to me,
Over the fields of glory,
Over the jasper sea.

2. Safe in the arms of Jesus,
   Safe from corroding care,
   Safe from the world's temptations;
   Sin cannot harm me there.
   Free from the blight of sorrow,
   Free from my doubts and fears;
   only a few more trials,
   only a few more tears!

Fanny had a visual disability, and experienced other breaking points, but her spiritual insight compensated for that lack. She became blind as a baby and was not able to see anything to miss, but as she grew, she probably missed doing all the activities of children her age. According to the quoted source, she wrote her first poem when she was at eight-year-old. The powerful words and messages of other songs such as "Blessed Assurance", "I shall know Him", and "Faith of our Fathers", plus others, show her spiritual insight. Those insights have challenged and blessed many Christian believers, and like she herself has said, "maybe if I had my sight, I would not have written those songs." We know that those songs have blessed and inspired many in their walk with God.

Every visually disabled person will not necessarily portray extraordinary talents, but God has given gifts to all His children, and He uses every life that is yielded to His control.

Read James 4:1,2

• How can you begin to work on your spiritual sight?

CHAPTER 17

*Yvonne: Disabled in order that she might help the disabled walk with God

God continues to condition and hone His people, just like parents will not cease to discipline their children. Yvonne is one of those people. My first impression when I first met her, was that she was clowning around. No wheelchair- bound young person exudes such joy of living and joviality. I expected her to quit the joke, laugh, stand up, and walk.

I'm still not sure what I expected of someone who was abled-bodied, but now confined, but I went away rebuked and challenged. Overall, Yvonne has that "there you are!" disposition.

Along with her joviality, Yvonne appreciates honesty, and likes the record to be straight. "I did not arrive at this disposition overnight, and besides, I have not arrived anywhere." She admits that she hitchhiked on her parents' faith for years, not grasping the importance of cultivating her own, and then, once she did that, her life changed in ways she still cannot believe.

Yvonne's family background piques interest, and transcends more than she is able to share. She comes from a large family who laughs their way through life, and wrestles problems to the ground. Like her siblings and other young people, she had dreams and

---

* Name changed

aspirations. She followed the right paths in Academia, and finally had her feet on the first rung of the ladder in her career. The rung, however broke.

It broke, even while she was still struggling with, and trying to figure out some of the ideas she'd heard while in university. There, her faith had taken many beatings, and she developed an uncertainty about her pitch among the volley ball game of new ideas and 'faiths 'being tossed around.

> "I was not certain whether it was a case where what I learned went against the grain of what I believed, or whether what I believed went against what was trending. Whatever the case, dichotomies were in place, and I had many questions regarding God and faith."

One Sunday morning as she joined many others in singing "To God be the glory", (one of Fanny Crosby's songs) the fact, the reminder that God did a great deed in sending Jesus, she knew she believed, and she surrendered her life to God. Her new found joy carried her through the next few months, and about two years later, one morning, Yvonne who usually sprang out of bed, was just too tired to get up for work. She however had to, so she forced herself to get up. Pain soon became an unwelcome, but constant companion.

Repeated medical tests could find no specific conclusive source, although it was evident that something was wrong. She began missing days from work, and subsequently could only manage part time, while she spent the other time in therapy. Her muscles and bones gradually stopped cooperating with the rest of her body, and before long, she had to use a wheelchair to get around. She was soon spending more time in the Doctor's office than anywhere else. Before long, an eight-hour work day was too much, it was out of the question, and she had to quit. She has had two major surgeries, and is now reconciled to the fact that she will never work at her career. The rungs became inaccessible and she could no longer climb.

> "My initial reaction", she admits, was, "Why is this happening? I have surrendered my life completely to God, and it seems He is rewarding me with health challenges."

Months of frustration and near despair followed. It did not make any sense at all to her. Why had she spent all that time studying and anticipating a career, only to quit working only two years on the job? Apart from God, family, was her main source of strength, and encouragement. She is also grateful for Christian friends.

While involved in therapy, Yvonne began to notice disabled people in a new way, especially those who are more disabled than she is. She has established a rapport with many, and is able to approach any, strike up a conversation, and share a laugh within a few minutes. She has a heart for disabled people, and has gained an audience where others would probably fail. This does not mean that only disabled people can be effective in reaching out to other disabled, Yvonne emphasizes with caution. Still, she believes that God permitted her situation so that when she speaks, her words carry more weight than those of someone who is not disabled. She also attributes her effectiveness to her ability to laugh at herself, and at life in general.

> "Moreover", she sums up her situation, "God disabled me so that I can reach out to those who are disabled and struggling with their circumstances."

Every case and situation is different just like each individual in the situations. God does not use carbon copy solutions. There is no solution that fits all except in the application of grace.

- What do you think about Yvonne's claim that God disabled her in order to use her to reach other disabled? Discuss.

CHAPTER 18

The Stronghearts*: Two cups of sorrow and more

Like other North American parents, as well as parents world-wide, Phillip and Alice Strongheart anticipated their children growing up and realizing their dreams. Above all else, they love and honor God, and introduced each of their three children to Him from an early age. The family became established, and all seemed to be going well, despite all the common occurrences. When their daughter Hope* began to manifest health problems, they had no undue concerns. They accepted the fact that they were not exempt from life's ups and downs.

Their concerns, however, began to grow when certain signs and symptoms appeared, lingered, and increased. Still they trusted God and continued to hope for the best. Their faith and trust in God strengthened their perseverance. They would need that more than they cared to imagine. Sorrow barged in them when they received Hope's prognosis, but Hope's sense of humor helped to succor them through those days of uncertainty. Family friends laughed, marvelling over her ability to joke about her predicament. Grief, however arrived blending with sorrow, and Alice and Phillip had to drink that cup, when Hope lost the battle with cancer at a young age.

That cup was a was a bitter one to drink, and the taste will not go away even when the severity decreases. Children usually bury their parents, not vice versa. And the fact that it happened to others, was no comfort. The family grieved even as they learned to get on with life minus one daughter, and their grief included a cycle of self-blame.

The joy over Margaret* their oldest child's marriage, and the subsequent arrival of grandchildren, diluted their sorrow for a season. Margaret's baby helped them to not really forget, but rather to handle their sorrow. The new life – God's gift to them, chased away the clouds of sorrow. But sorrow soon barged in again when Margaret began to manifest signs and symptoms similar to Hope's. Problems increased rather than decrease with interventions, and they learned that they would have to drink from sorrow's cup once again, when the family heard the prognosis.

Even when she was aware of her condition, Margaret maintained calmness. In fact, she often requested prayers for others with similar health problems. And although Phillip and Alice knew that she would eventually die from her illness; the time of her home going was nonetheless a surprise, and produced pain. They once again experienced – tasted grief, when twenty years after Hope's home going, Margaret went too. Their path has been marked with pain and other difficulties. Questions which they realize no one can answer, riddled their minds and filled their days. They also realize that God does not have to answer any of those questions.

> "Initially, self-blame was strong, and it was only our trust in God kept us going after Hope died, and it is that same trust that continues to keep us going after Margaret died too", Alice admits.

> "I often worried my mind, wondering if I could have done more to prevent both of them from dying", Phillip added. "Overall, he concluded, "God has a purpose, He alone knows why he allowed us two of our three children. And although we neither know the answers, nor understand His ways, we have to keep believing that He knows best."

God chose to, and pulled back the veil a little, and while the Stronghearts warn against this as an explanation, and also against expecting this to be the norm, they are joyful and thankful that at Hope's funeral, two people confessed faith in God. It is a great encouragement to them.

"If we had to drink that cup, in order for one soul to turn to God, then it was worth it, despite the sorrow involved", Phillip concluded.

The Stronghearts, by trusting God, believe that their daughters' deaths have helped to strengthen their faith. Every case is different, and likewise, everyone's perspective. While we can all learn something from each other's suffering and grief, God will not necessarily work in the same way in every life. But He will work, if we allow Him.

- What is the level of your conviction at this point?

CHAPTER 19

Frances: Knocked down, in order that I may become steadfast – and the work goes on.

Like drivers who sometimes attempt to run their vehicles on empty, I often run on faith and feelings, rather than on faith alone. I am learning that this does not mean that I just hope for the best, sit back and do nothing. I once held that stance. It reminds me of some humorous (only in retrospect) situations while I was on the mission field. Some taxi drivers would get only enough diesel to take them a short distance. The vehicle would of course, stall, and then they would get just enough for another short distance; then repeat the process. How much like that, I have often behaved. I am, however learning that "without faith, I cannot please God", just like the taxis would come to a halt, without diesel. I am also learning that I cannot, and must not depend upon feelings. They do have their place, but lack the reliability one needs on life's battlefield.

Instead of exercising faith, I often allow opinions to affect my outlook, and consequently my behavior. Faith soars occasionally, like it did while I prepared to serve on the Mission field. But while I was there, I realized that I'd taken extra baggage: doubts and fears which often hampered and barred my effectiveness. Another important lesson: I cannot bring praise to God without active faith. It may be small, but its presence and activity are sufficient. I agree with a speaker's words "Fear prevents us from focusing on God's character, but when we exercise faith, it ousts fear as we once again focus on who He is."[17] This resonates with the struggles in my life.

David, in one of his Psalms declares: "My heart is *steadfast*, I will sing and give praise."[18] Those words often convict my heart, how I longed to know stability, but instead of allowing God's Holy Spirit to do the work, I often despaired over ever attaining to that. God, however, shewed leniency toward me when, for example, I sensed His leading to serve in cross-cultural ministries, and my faith sprouted wings as I practised His admonition: "Be still and know that I am God."[19] At that time recession was rife, and being me, I focused on situations, but as my mentors encouraged me, I looked to God. I saw His hand, as He provided full support in less than a year, yet on the mission field I took my eyes off Jesus repeatedly, and when I did, faith plummeted. I failed to focus on God's character, and like Peter, I looked at the waves of circumstances around me. Some of those circumstances included feelings that I was not really a good missionary, also that as a single woman; I had missed out on some of the happiness in life, but had most of all, failed as God's child. All this plus other issues, knocked me into waves of despair in which I almost drowned at times. Ongoing family issues soon necessitated the need to take a leave of absence from the mission field. But like Jacob and Moses did, I manipulated certain situations in my effort to bring about the happiness and fulfillment I craved in secret.

Much of my motive for taking a break from the mission field, included situations related to feelings. My main motive was to help care for my mother, but I also hoped that a relationship would lead to marriage. I had certain expectations of God. I was hoping that He would, actually I felt He owed it to me, to compensate me for unresolved hurts. He does not have to, and He did not. It does not mean that He is not mindful, or that He does not care. His ways are far above mine, and it is only in retrospect that I am glad and grateful that He did not. I soon realized that I was forcing open a closed door, and might have opened a Pandora's box. This was the case of "William, The Would-be Conqueror and Pasty the Fool."[19]

Patsy loved God, (she still does with all her heart) and was serving Him in the area which He directed, and despite a few challenges, she loved the work. She struggled with one particular problem, however. She felt God should make it up to her, compensate her for heartaches she'd experienced throughout childhood, and well into her young adult years. She refused to believe that God would allow disappointments and heartaches to become the only experiences that came anywhere close to her expectations from life, and from God specifically. The Mission field was not promising in that area, so Patsy became resigned to her state.

Then one day, William appeared, and wanted to take her to his kingdom. A friendship sprouted. She experienced uncertainties about God's will in the request, but dared to hope it may be of Him. Friends and colleagues, however were sure that was not a path from God, but Patsy was a little afraid to let go. Signs and indications that it was not of God, continued to abound. Many opined with honesty and love that they saw a red light, and tried to deter her, but she went against the red light, fearing that she might be passing up her last chance. She even visited William's kingdom, and while she was there, more indications – red lights, were evident, yet Patsy held out.

She left on a leave of absence, and shortly after returning home, she continued to hope for that dream to become reality. God, however slammed the door shut and she finally acquiesced, and repented of her behavior. Patsy now thanks God, and her friends for saving her from becoming William's conquered fool. While she rests in God's will, Patsy still had occasional moments when she relived the past."[20]

I once again allowed feelings to overrule, and I gave in to grief, feeling bad over what I had done, while feeling that I had lost the last opportunity for at least one mode of fulfilment. I cringe in shame now at my hypocrisy, and especially at the lies I used to sing. The songs themselves are not lies, rather it was my failure to practice what I claimed in words and emotions. Faith continued to plunge, and I became concerned when friends and family members tried to dissuade me against this negative habit. I was especially saddened that I may have caused others to doubt because of my weak faith, and my hypocrisy. I continued in the snare of feeling awful about it. I was like a gerbil on a treadmill.

One Sunday, a sermon stirred and provoked me to ask God to shake me for the sake of becoming more like Jesus. I'd made similar, but empty promises before, but God took me at my words, and that time, He allowed, and orchestrated situations which at first seemed like invasions, but later I allowed them to help me to see what was in my heart. And what I saw was not good. I'd been working as an RN on a medical unit, and as I reflect on it now, much of my performance was based on feelings. Inferiority and fears were outstanding, ongoing problems, among others. I thrived on people's positive opinions of me, and on good reports, but was often, still afraid that I was not good enough, and also that something would go wrong. This affected my work. For example, I was so anxious, and so keen on a good record, that I arrived at work fifteen minutes early so I could get a head start.

In retrospect, I derived much satisfaction from the opinion that I was a *good* nurse, and that became a great percentage of my status. I did not know it then, and maybe I would not have admitted it, if someone had pointed it out. Actually some colleagues did that. Most of those who did, exercised grace and kindness when they told me I did not need to be perfect. I was unwittingly worshipping my status, and what I felt commended me to people. Alongside all that, I had the grasshopper mentality, where everyone was better than I was, so probably the status of a good nurse would boost me. I was not aware that I was not focusing on God's character.

Shortly after my request that God would shake me, He did, but not in the way I expected; although I still cannot say what I expected Him to do. That included losing my job, and unemployment exacerbated situations. I denied God's hand in it. How could that happen? And How could God allow that to happen? What do I do now? I despaired after months of fruitless efforts to find another job. Meanwhile, I sought comfort and assurance from others. I sought solace from people, rather than pouring out my heart before God. Feelings became dictators, and my fears increased each time I internalized negative feedbacks about age being a factor in my inability to find a job.

A year later, I was still searching, and after much introspection, reflection, and evaluation; situations appeared to be improving. There was a possibility of at least one job, but a few weeks later, back and hip pain, which neither painkillers nor massage therapy changed, finally propelled me to the emergency room. Long story short, I had a slipped disc. Pain and fear became constant companions. Mix these with doubts and guilt, and that described my existence. I dreaded the thought, and feared I would never walk again. What is God doing to me? I often wondered.

Surgery helped to ease the pain, but during the six months while I was on the waiting list, pain restricted my activities, some movements and had me under apartment arrest. Pride, a cousin I do not like, visited often, and influenced humiliation: Just look at you, with a cane. Defiance appeared out of nowhere, actually out of my heart: Surely I'm not at that stage yet. I do not want to be at that stage, I lamented. However, God convicted me with the realization that I had the time to give more thoughts to passages I was reading from a read- through-the-Bible program. His words took on new dimensions, became more alive. I learned to internalise truth, get rid of lies, and put everything in proper perspective. A battle ensued. I had begun to feel sorry for myself and that was an ongoing battle, along with feelings of guilt over what I perceived not only as locust eaten years, but a locust eaten life. Fear of the future, especially fear of surgery, and fear that I may not walk again compounded the situation.

However, God continued to mete out grace and patience in abundant measures toward me. He also used various other means to get my attention – to show me that I needed to get aligned with His will. While visiting a friend in her senior residence one day, the lesson from a simple incident helped me to see the need to examine my heart closer.

Another friend *Ladie, and I had just finished supper with our mutual friend Jewel, and were preparing for tea and a game. While we prepared, *Jewel bewailed the loss of a "special coffee mug, with beautiful butter-flies". I remembered seeing the mug, and pointed out the fact that one of the mugs: the one she would use, looked just like it, but she denied it. Moreover, she feared she might have left it somewhere, and we empathised with her loss, while trying to prompt her memory of the last place she possibly used it. She could not recall.

I began pouring the hot liquid into the mugs, pouring hers first. After a few seconds, Ladie exclaimed: "Didn't you say you lost your mug?

"You didn't. It's right here." There was the mug Jewel thought she had lost, and there were the beautiful butterflies. Dessert and the game were suspended for a while, as we celebrated the fact that she'd not lost it. We also realized what was happening.

The chemicals in the mug's compound, reacted with the heat from the hot liquid, bringing out the bright colors. We laughed about it, but what a timely and practical lesson that was for me. Just like heat brought out the true colors on the mug, so the heat from trials and hardships – unemployment, giving up what I thought was an investment, plus severe pain, had exposed my true color – the contents of my heart. Trials had squeezed my heart, and its content leaked. I failed the test.

I'd been struggling with unemployment, and the loss of my nurse role – my status. Therefore, looming surgery and its prospects were not uplifting subjects, as far as I was concerned. That lesson, however, plus my friends' love, fellowship and overall support that evening, gave me much to reconsider, although I often fell again into the mud of despair.

Just recently I heard more truths which I appreciate: (although hearing them initially was akin to taking Mefloquine, a brand of Quinine; the epitome of bitter taste) "God, in His sovereignty and wisdom, knocks down things in our lives. And sometimes He knocks down the good things, as well as the bad."[21]

CHAPTER 20

Just about the time I was awaiting surgery, God showed me that I needed heart surgery, and He was the only one to do it. He began by using another friend's probing and timely questions to help me to come to terms with the entire situation. 'Do you think God's hand is in this? Do you think He is aware?' She asked after a heart leak, including complaints about my pain, my embarrassment of unemployment, my feeling of uselessness, and my fear of the future. Despite much encouragement and advice, I had been still struggling with the idea about God's hand in my situation, while being cognizant of the fact, that some of the hardships I encountered was just "life kicking us in the teeth", as one Pastor liked to interpret it. I wondered why God would allow me to lose my job at a time I needed it. I realized also, and now confess that losing my job included faults – my faults. But he could have prevented it, yet did not.

When I finally acceded to the fact that God's hand was in it, certain facts began to line up: God shook me like I requested, although I was not completely willing for Him to have His own way. I was like a child with candies, and I preferred them to real food. As God asked me to give all to Him, I clutched them tighter, but He gently pried them from my grasp. First it was my job, then my house, and oh no, please not my health.

I can tolerate almost anything else as long as I am in good health. I realized with sorrow, and had to admit, that it was not really "all for Jesus" like I thought it was. Fear is also a big issue. I've struggled with fear all my life, and need to let go of it. I am learning more about fear. I am learning that it is focus on self, and every time I allow fear to overcome me; I am saying in effect that I cannot rely on God. I'm also learning that fear is not the real culprit, rather it is my reaction – how I deal with fear. Everyone experiences a measure of fear, but most people do not allow it to dominate them. Fear shows that I am functioning at surface level.

In my struggle with fear, I often backpedal, but while I still struggle, I am no longer on the mat in the wrestling. I grieve, and confess now that fear prevented me from accomplishing all that I could have. I used to find it easier to hide behind fear, than it is was to face the disciplines. Everyone faces opposition, unpleasant opinions, and other situations which are normal hurdles with which we contend on ambition's pathway. I am often like the man in the Proverbs who will not go out, because, "there is a lion in the way." That lion in my way, is fear. I do not put God always before me like I should. Rather I am focused on self. Fear does not portray steadfastness of heart – a quality I need. God declares in His word that He has not given (me) a spirit of bondage to fear, but one of power, love, and a sound mind." I lack this, and I want it! In my struggle with fear, especially over the last three years, I put together, what I like to describe as the a to zed of fear:

Awakens anxiety
Belittles God's words and His promises
Cancels praise
Dilutes joy
Entangles the mind
Flirts with scepticism
Gorges on negativity
Harasses rationality
Invades the heart
Jeopardizes confidence
Kills motivation
Loathes faith
Misdirects thoughts
Negates trust

Oppresses the spirit
Paralyzes goals
Quells enthusiasm
Restricts growth
Scorns optimism
Terrorizes the soul
Undermines God's presence
Vandalizes hope
Waives common sense
Zaps energy

This is exactly what fear was doing in my life, but If I only talk about it, without changing my behavior, it is akin to placing a container to catch water from a leaky roof. I may seek to save one spot from becoming discolored, but the real problem is the hole in the roof. Unless I fix that, I have not really started to tackle the problem. The damage increases. Unless I get rid of – overcome my fears, the hole in my faith will remain, and will leak and damage every area of my life. The following is another lesson in poem that I use, to remind myself of fear's destructive force.

Be aware of fear
the fore-runner of despair
our very sense of God's presence
over time it will impair

Fear will make us see
That which is not there
We forget
That God is near

And that is our enemy's doing
who by the way; is the greatest liar
listening to him
leaves us in a mire.

We must never
let him charm us
Nor should we
Let him disarm us [22]

As I examine my life, especially the ease and speed in which I give in to fear, I despair over making it to the finish line, but God is not finished with me yet, and I am glad and thankful for that fact. He permits trials in my life, and particular problems like job loss, so that I can see what is in my heart. Some readers may not understand this, but I sense that God had to dash me to pieces – allowed circumstances to force me to think about some behaviors. "Now consider this you who forget God, lest I tear you to pieces, and there is none to deliver; Whoever offers praise glorifies me; and to him who orders his conduct aright I will show the salvation of God" (Psalm 50:22)

My breaking point started when I was left with nothing. Specifically, I do not like basement apartments, but there I was in one, instead of my condominium. Was there a lesson I needed to learn about contentment? I also always enjoyed near to perfect health, yet there I was hobbling, needing to use a walking aid. Was that yet another lesson I needed to learn? A lesson about contentment in all situations including ill-health? My reaction at the time, however was: How could God allow this? What is He doing? pride prodded and propelled me to ask when my eyes were not focused on Jesus.

CHAPTER 21

I am now in the process of *learning* that Jesus is all I need. There are still times when I desire to have my own way – take a break from carrying my cross – bypass the disciplines. My soul grieves when I consider the lost years – those "locust eaten years", and I cry out to God to salvage what can be salvaged. He promised long ago that He would restore to His people, the locust eaten years, and those years in bondage due to rebellion. As I think about this, I think of Moses. I earlier intimated that I appreciate him, and I do so because I can relate to many of his experiences, and especially his mistakes – his shortcomings.

- He tried to again help God – manipulated situations.
- Compulsion drove him at times, although his intentions were good
- He tried to help God out: tried to manipulate situations.
- He knew fear, and allowed it to become a dictator. As a result, he ran from his problems, instead of running to God.
- He became resigned to his situation too easily.
- He did not think he had the qualifications, nor did he think he was ready when God thought he was.
- He was at times focused on what others thought of him, and in doing so he limited himself, and God.

- To some (especially in today's world) his age would be a problem, and he would not even be considered as a candidate for the task. He was old, yet God called and used him.
- After his attempted argument with God, Moses dared to face his fears, when he re-entered Egypt, and faced the Pharaoh.

Of all the points about Moses' mistakes, I particularly appreciate the last one, because I too, struggle with fears. I am not claiming that now I know – that I have more ready answers. If anyone should happen to scrutinize my behavior on any given day, he/she would right away know that I still have much to learn. Furthermore, I am a slow learner but I am grateful that God is a wonderful teacher – the greatest teacher. He does not allow me to slip by with lessons I fail to learn, and neither does he condemn me. Rather, He lets me repeat lessons I have failed to grasp, He turns up the heat, bringing about situations which expedite changes, until I learn. I am becoming more aware, that this will take a lifetime.

What I do know is a certainty, is this: God continues to teach me, and I need to keep learning to be a good listener. This trait lacks constancy in my life. I sometimes run ahead and perform against my conviction, putting out His Holy Spirit's fire. When I listen well, I will hear, and He will make me effective – more like Jesus. And that is something that I desire more than anything else. God's word tells me that "He chastens – disciplines each of His children. Also, "no discipline at present seems to be joyful, but painful (a thousand ouches to that) nevertheless, afterward, it yields the peaceable fruit of righteousness to those who have been trained by it." [23] God had to turn up the heat in my life. I still have much training to accomplish. I hope He will not need to turn up the heat any more. Meanwhile, I often forget lessons because I fail to practice what I learn. The next poem is another lesson I learned while I was temporarily immobilized by pain as I awaited surgery.

I agree to an extent, with the statement "God screams at us through our pain." It is not in the same manner or mood in which people do it to each other. Scripture declares that parents (who are not perfect) discipline us for their own good, but God who is perfect, does it for our good. My mother applied physical correction when after several other forms of discipline, my siblings, and I especially, still refused to listen. That physical action spoke louder than words did in that setting. When we fail to listen, when we do not pay attention, God for our good, allows trials which causes us to question and ponder life in a new way. Those questions may at first be edged with defiance and lack of faith, but as we learn to be calm, the questions become more mature.

> The anvil of our Master's will
> Is often like the Dentist's drill
> We find it difficult to be still
> To let His ways our beings fill
>
> But unlike the Dentist who gives Novocain
> To offer comfort, to deaden the pain
> Our master's love is the only sedation
> It's for our good, it's not condemnation.
>
> The noises and sensations in our ears
> Are often disquieting, arousing fears
> And although at times, the pain brings tears
> He aims for Godly characters.[23]

I have also over the last few years especially, appreciated Steve Green's song which echoes the cry of my heart. I do realize that it is an ongoing battle between the flesh and the Spirit, and it will never cease, even when I am learning to rest in God.

> "There burns a fire with sacred heat
> White hot with holy flame
> And all who dare pass through the blaze will not emerge the same
> Some as bronze and some as silver
> Some as gold but through great skill
> All are hammered by their suffering
> On the anvil of His will.

The refiner's fire, has now become my soul's desire
Purged and cleansed and purified
That the Lord be glorified
He is consuming my soul
Refining me, making me whole
No matter what I may lose
I choose the refiner's fire.

I'm learning now to trust His touch
To crave the fire's embrace
For though my past with sins are etched
His mercies did erase
Each time His purging cleanses deeper
I'm not sure that I'll survive
Yet the strength in growing weaker
Keeps my hungry soul alive."[24]

God heard, answered, and turned up the heat, and there are times, when "Each time the purging cleanses deeper, I'm not sure that I'll survive, yet the strength in growing weaker, keeps my hungry soul alive." I do not ever want to run into a worse situation through self-help and manipulation. It seems God keeps turning up the heat, and I would lie if I say there is anything pleasant about the process. I must, however, allow God to continue working on me, to remove the tarnish, to bring about necessary changes, despite the discomforts involved. I am learning also to view my belongings as a loan form God, just something to help me function, and He can reclaim them without notice anytime. I once thought that was my stance until recently.

When I lost my job, I had to change my living accommodations, and needed to put most of my belongings in storage. When I moved to another city to search for a job, I had to leave them behind. Lives and situation change inevitably, and developing situations dictated that I make other arrangements. When I opened, actually as soon as I approached some of the containers, I realized that mice and squirrels preceded me, thus legitimizing the need for those arrangements. Those four-footed (thieves I want to call them, but in retrospect, I view them as) *teachers* used much of my belongings as maternity wards, and hotel accommodations.

Much was beyond repair, and had to go. "Lay not up for yourselves treasures on earth where moth and dust destroy, and where thieves break through and steal"[25] (in this case *where mice and squirrels gnaw through*) entered my mind with clarity. Along with the spoilage of my belongings, was the somber fact of closure – the closure of a phase of my life.

I am *learning* to connect with God through all this, and through prayer, I continue to investigate and discover what He wants to put in place of the things He knocked over – shook out of my life. He is under no obligation to tell me anything, and although it concerns me, it is none of my business. He may not even replace anything, and He may never let me understand why. It is, however, my business is to trust Him and obey Him, and I need to practice both for balance.

I am still under construction, and I often mess up. I drop the baton repeatedly, and even after I have pleaded with God to salvage what He can from this wrecked vessel, I spoil the pattern that He is remolding. I want Him to cool the refining fire a little. But I know that like gems in the making, He must chip here, chisel there, and shape until I am perfect in His sight – not mine or others. There is hope. Forgiveness is only a prayer of confession and repentance away.

- How about you? Is God turning up the heat in your life?
- How will you respond?

*This indicates name change, which I have used to protect privacy, although the characters were willing to share their stories.

My own story is a part of my story. William exists, and I was almost the almost Patsy (one easily fooled) I am in no way seeking to belittle William. The gist of the story is to show how easily I can fall away from God, if I do not remain focused. The poems, except Wit's End Corner, are those I penned, and which I hope will portray my heart's response to truths and lessons God has been teaching me over the years.

Endnotes

1   The Free Dictionary June 2014
2   Encyclopedia.com September 2015
3   Ephesians 2:10
4   Cefrey, Holly A summary of Gems Rosen House of Publishing, New York
5   Romans 15:4
6   An old Chinese proverbs
7   Wilson, Antoinette Wits End Corner 1912
8   Psalm 119:67
9   Isaiah 58:16
10   Celfrey, Holly A Summary of Gems Rosen Publishing House, New York
11   Psalm 105:11-16
12   Sermon notes Metropolitan Bible Church, Ottawa, Ontario, Canada
13   1 Samuel 2:6,7
14   Internet download January 2015
15   Sermon notes Metropolitan Bible Church Ottawa, Ontario, Canada
16   Proverbs 4:23
17   Internet download January 2015
18   Psalm 57:7
19   Psalm 46:10
20   My story
21   Sermon notes from Metropolitan Bible Church Ottawa Ontario, Canada
22   Fear: Poem by Frances, Patsy Wilson July 2015
23   Brokenness: Poem by Frances, Patsy Wilson January 2015
24   Green, Steve The Refiner's Fire 1989
25   Matthew 26:19

Printed in the United States
By Bookmasters